This book belongs to

_____

This book is dedicated to the individuals who I have had the honor to collaborate with: Kang Nhin, our small but mighty teams at Ninja Life Hacks and Nhinja Sushi, the team at F.A.I.T.H. Kids, UCO Department of Entrepreneurship Board of Advisors, Greater OKC Asian Chamber of Commerce Founding Board of Advisors, Collective for Children Founding Board of Advisors

Copyright © 2024 Grow Grit Press LLC. All rights reserved. No part of this book may be reproduced in any form without permission in writing from the publisher. Please send bulk order requests to info@ninjalifehacks.tv

Paperback ISBN: 979-8-89614-001-6
Hardcover ISBN: 979-8-89614-003-0
eBook ISBN: 979-8-89614-002-3

Printed and bound in the USA.
NinjaLifeHacks.tv

Ninja Life Hacks®
by Mary Nhin

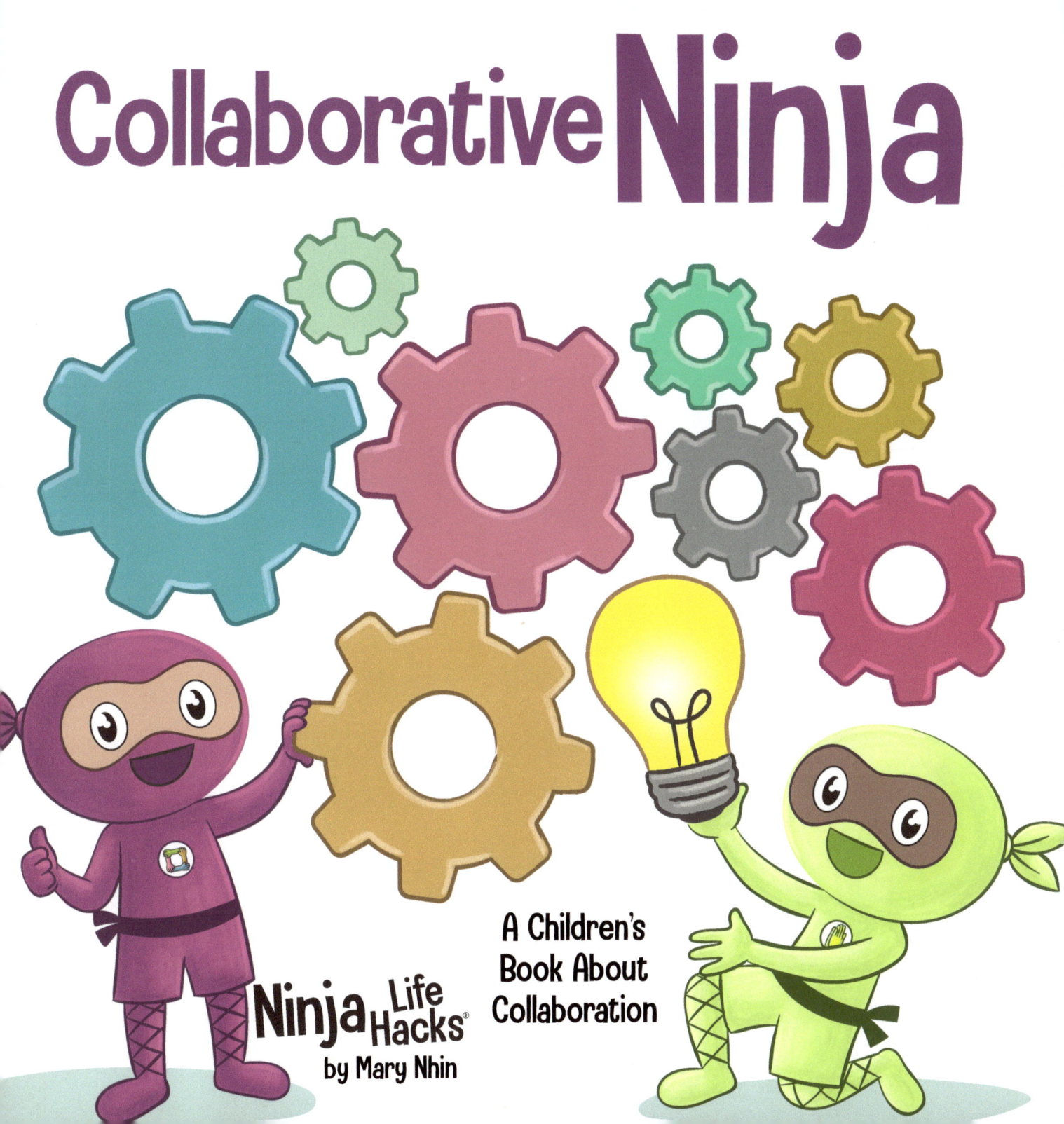

Once, during a group activity, we couldn't agree on what to do. I felt frustrated, and we didn't get much done. I didn't know how to work as a team, and it made me feel really unsure.

I realized that teamwork makes the dream work! Now, when I work with others, I know how to collaborate and make it a great experience for everyone.

WE DID IT TOGETHER!

www.ingramcontent.com/pod-product-compliance
Lightning Source LLC
LaVergne TN
LVHW070437070526
838199LV00015B/529